JAMIE'S TURN

Story by Jamie DeWitt
Illustrations by Julie Brinckloe

A Carnival Press Book   Raintree Publishers Inc.

Published by Raintree Publishers Inc.
330 East Kilbourn Avenue, Milwaukee, Wisconsin 53202.

Art Direction: Su Lund

Text copyright © 1984, Raintree Publishers Inc.
Illustrations copyright © 1984, Julie Brinckloe

Printed in the United States of America   1 2 3 4 5 6 7 8 9 0 88 87 86 85 84

Library of Congress Cataloging in Publication Data
DeWitt, Jamie.   Jamie's turn.   "A Carnival Press book."
Summary: The author describes how, at the age of eleven, he rescued his stepfather after an accident with farm machinery and how he helped to keep the farm running until his stepfather recovered nearly a year later.   1. Farm life—Juvenile literature. 2. Corn picking machinery—Accidents—Juvenile literature. 3. DeWitt, Jamie—Juvenile literature. 4. Children's writings.
[1. Accidents. 2 Stepfathers. 3. Farm life. 4. Children's writings] I. Brinckloe, Julie, ill. II. Title. III. Series.
S519.D49 1984   630   84-13973   ISBN 0-940742-37-3

*T*o my stepfather, Butch Raines,
and to my teacher, Lonnie Miller.

—J. D.

*F*or Pamela.

—J. B.

When I was eleven, my stepdad got hurt.
My stepdad's name is Butch. My name is Jamie.
At that time, we didn't know each other very well.

It was autumn, and Butch was picking corn. Our corn picker was old. The corn fields were all in the valley near our farm.

I was riding with Butch on the side of the tractor.
We had picked one field. And then we started
to open another field. We were picking the outside
row of corn.

When we got halfway around the field, the corn
picker plugged up. So I jumped off the tractor.

Butch began to get off. The power-takeoff shaft of the corn picker grabbed the clothes on his leg. It started to rip off his clothes.

Butch started swinging and hollering
for me. So I ran to the tractor, jumped
on, and pushed in the clutch. I shut off
the power-takeoff shaft.

9

Then I ran to the house for help. When Mom heard me, she knew that there was something wrong.

Mom and I got in the truck. Tom, a friend who was staying with us, saw us going quickly to the corn field. So he ran to meet us at the corn picker.

We had a blanket and pillows in the truck. We used them to cover up Butch.

Then Mom and I hopped in the truck and went back to the house to call the ambulance. Tom stayed with Butch to keep him awake.

Mom went back to the corn field after she made the phone call. I stayed with my new baby brother and two sisters. The girls, Tara and Bobbie, were crying.

I just held it in. But I was nervous.

Tom was standing out by the road when the
ambulance came. The driver didn't want to go into
the field because of the mud. But Tom got him to go.
   One of the neighbors had seen the ambulance go by.
He took one of his tractors to the field.

When the ambulance began to drive out, it got stuck in the mud. Our neighbor pulled out the ambulance with his tractor.

The ambulance took off, and Mom followed behind it in the car.

Tom brought the truck back to the house. Then Tom and I started chores. Another neighbor came over to help us milk the cows.

After milking, we went to bed.

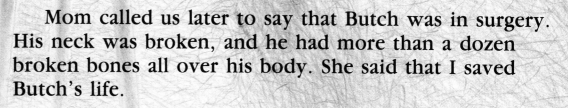

Mom called us later to say that Butch was in surgery. His neck was broken, and he had more than a dozen broken bones all over his body. She said that I saved Butch's life.

The next day, there was a corn bee on our farm; people came to help pick the rest of our corn. There were more than five corn pickers.

Uncle Donny took the tractor that Butch had been using for picking back to the shed.

Aunt Donna cooked for everybody. By six o'clock
that night, they had picked all of the corn.
 Mom called my grandmother and told her to take me
out of school so that I could visit Butch. But Bobbie
and Tara could not see him yet.

214

I went to La Crosse to see Butch in the hospital. He was lying in bed. He couldn't smoke, and he couldn't even talk very well.

A week later, my sisters and I went back to see Butch. There were also several relatives and other people in his room, so we had to be quiet.

About an hour after we left, the nurses prepared
Butch for more surgery. He had pins put in his toes and
a plate put in his arm.

During the next three months, Butch had at least ten
more operations. He had to stay in the hospital the
whole time.

While Butch was in the hospital, I was doing his work on the farm. Twice a day I milked the cows. I cleaned the milking machines, fed the cows and calves, cleaned the stalls, and kept the barn in good shape.

I also took care of the pigs. I fed them morning and night. I got the grain that we needed to feed all of our livestock ready for the feed mill.

Butch came home at the end of the winter. He couldn't do anything yet. He had to have his arm rubbed every four hours. His leg had to be exercised, too.

Even though the doctors didn't think that he'd ever walk again, Butch was walking soon. He had a limp. His foot was still hurt badly. And he was able to move his arm in some directions.

After a year, Butch was able to do all of the chores. But he still had three more operations to go, on his arm and toes.

The experience has helped me to grow up. And I'm more aware of farm safety now.

I became closer to my stepdad. I have respect for him; he went through a lot. He's a brave man.

And he's proud of me, because I saved his life and because I had to do a man's job for a year.

Butch bought me a motorbike. I love it.

This true adventure of Jamie DeWitt's family took place near Ontario, Wisconsin, a town of about 400 people. The Kickapoo River Valley runs near Ontario. It has made the land beautiful, with picturesque cliffs and valleys. The land tends to make farming difficult, though. Still, Jamie and his family are able to support themselves by working on their 64-acre dairy farm.

Jamie has two younger stepsisters, Tara and Bobbie Jo, and a younger half brother, Clay. And he has a newly born half sister, Kayla. Along with his mother, Karen, and stepfather, Butch, the entire family is very proud of Jamie for having his story published as a book. That was part of winning first prize in Raintree's 1984 *Publish-a-Book Contest.*

The other part of winning first prize was receiving money. Jamie used some of it to buy heifers for the farm.

Jamie was twelve when his story was entered into the contest. He had worked on it at Ontario Grade School with his teacher, Lonnie Miller. Since Jamie has a learning disability that makes it difficult for him to write down what he is thinking, he began by dictating his story to Mrs. Miller. Judy Stedman, the school librarian, sent in Jamie's story along with others from Ontario Grade School.

Jamie DeWitt's book, *Jamie's Turn*, is the winner of the first prize in Raintree's 1984 *Publish-a-Book Contest.* His story was chosen from entries that came from all over the United States and some other parts of the world. Fourth-, fifth-, and sixth-grade students entered the contest.

The twenty second-prize winners of the contest were Juliette Buerkle, Lake Worth, Florida; Jonathan Burns, Valdosta, Georgia; Karen Clayton, Lexington, North Carolina; Steve Cooper, Moro, Illinois; Penelope Degadillo, Foster City, California; Arden S. Durham, Marietta, Georgia; Ann W. Eberle, Newington, Connecticut; Liza Fiorentino, Madison, Connecticut; Janelle Marie Guenther, Greene, Iowa; Jimmy Hill, Chatham, Illinois; Jason Kobes, Belmond, Iowa; Layli Koontz, Bethel, Alaska; Molly Loughlin, Mystic, Connecticut; David Nelson, Schenectady, New York; Dylan Nelson, Sullivan's Island, South Carolina; Sara Nichols, Woodinville, Washington; Tracey Stone, Lake Havasu City, Arizona; Dawn Charlotte Tappy, Fredonia, Wisconsin; Van Thai, Westminster, California; and Amy Joan Wiemerslage, Dorchester, Iowa.

Julie Brinckloe was born in Mare Island, California. She received a bachelor of fine arts degree from Carnegie-Mellon University in 1972. Ms. Brinckloe has illustrated many stories and poems, including *The Bollo Caper* by Art Buchwald and *Lotta on Troublemaker Street* by Astrid Lindgren. She is the author and illustrator of *The Spider Web, Gordon Goes Camping,* and *Gordon's House.* She currently lives in New York.